Beyond Limits

Stories of Victory, Triumph, & Success

———————

Compiled by Dr. Aleta V. Ashford

DEDICATION

This book is dedicated to Sarah Michael, the sister of fellow author Sue Michael Carter, who passed away unexpectedly in 2024 during the course of this project. In the midst of her grief, Sue discovered the strength and courage to persist on her journey, honoring her sister by choosing to embrace a vibrant life each day. This work serves as a heartfelt celebration of her sister's memory.

In Loving Memory of Sarah Michael
February 2, 1943-July 31, 2024

Table Of Contents

1. The Gift of Friendship   5

2. Embracing Today!   14

3. Rising From the Shadows   23

4. Walking In Faith   33

5. Victory Through Adversity   42

6. Defining Success   49

7. God's Unwavering Love   57

8. Your Purpose Awaits   66

9. A Light To Guide Us Home   73

FOREWORD

When I was asked to write the foreword for Beyond Limits, my first thought was, "I have never written a foreword before; is she sure she'd want me to do this?" My second thought was, "Of course she's sure, probably because she knows I haven't done this before."

If there's one person who can make you feel like you've got this—even when you clearly don't—it's Dr. Aleta V. Ashford. After collecting my thoughts, I felt a wave of pride and gratitude and began to write what came to mind.

This book, a testament to the strength and resilience of women from all walks of life, perfectly represents who Dr. Ashford is. She is not only a key contributor but is also an embodiment of what this book is about: that no obstacle is too great to overcome when met with faith, determination, and courage.

To the world, Dr. Ashford is a powerhouse. Not only is she a professor, but she is also a successful corporate professional who has forged a path in both fields coupled with having earned her master's and a doctoral degree in business. As the founder of Incessant Publishing, LLC, she has amplified voices and stories that deserve to be heard, launching her first book through this venture in 2018. She is the creator of a globally impactful training series and a certified CPR instructor. Her work has taken her across the world, sharing knowledge and inspiring others to lead as boldly as she does.

To me, Dr. Ashford is much more than these impressive accomplishments. She is more than the college professor, the newspaper columnist, or the talented podcaster. She is my aunt. She is my role model, my inspiration, my anchor, and my best friend. She is a woman who has been my unwavering supporter in every endeavor I have pursued. She is the one who cheers the loudest and prays the hardest. She is someone who embodies grace, strength, and resilience in every aspect of her life.

Even when weathering her own storms, she still finds a way to be an anchor for others who are suffering through their own personal storms. Watching her navigate challenges and achieve extraordinary success has profoundly shaped who I am today. I am beyond grateful to have gone through the things I have gone through with my aunt by my side. She has not only been a guiding light but also a reminder that even the toughest battles can be won with faith and perseverance—and sometimes with just the word "no."

To my sister and me, she is nothing short of amazing, and we are endlessly proud of the woman she is and all the glass ceilings she has broken along the way.

My aunt's role as Super Mom to my cousin, who is now thriving in college, is another testament to her strength and love. She has poured her heart into raising a kind, intelligent, and capable young man, and she has done so with grace (a lot of grace) and humility. Her journey as a mother exemplifies the challenges and triumphs that define her character. Her journey to becoming "Dr. A" alone would require a book of its own.

The title of this book, Beyond Limits, is a perfect reflection of Dr. Ashford's journey and the lives of the women whose journeys are shared within these pages. Dr. Ashford's faith serves as the foundation for everything she does—like being the founder of Grounded Jeremiah 29:11, a faith-based women's ministry made up of over 10,000 women! Her belief that there is a divine plan for each of us, one of hope and a future, is not only inspiring but also transformative for those fortunate enough to know her. Through her hard work and dedication, she has brought women together to share their experiences, support one another, and grow in faith—a mission that beautifully aligns with the essence of this book.

What makes Dr. Ashford's story—and this book—so powerful is the emotional depth and authenticity behind every word. This isn't just a book about overcoming adversity; it's a celebration of what it means to rise above circumstances that seem impossible, and it's written by women just like you and me.

This book is also about the beautiful process of rising above, the power of hope, community, and the audacity to dream bigger. It is a beacon for anyone who has ever felt like the odds were stacked against them and a reminder that, with determination and faith, anything is possible!

Beyond Limits is a written testament to the incredible resilience of women who refused to be defined by their circumstances. They are proof that success isn't just about achieving goals; it's about the journey, the lessons learned along the way, and the courage to keep moving forward.

Dr. Aleta V. Ashford has dedicated her life to uplifting others, whether through her professional endeavors, her writing, teaching, her faith-based works, or her role as a mother, wife, mentor, and friend. Her ability to connect with people on an emotional level, to inspire them to see beyond their limits, and to encourage them to dream bigger is nothing short of remarkable.

To my aunt, thank you for being you. Thank you for showing my sister and I what it means to dream big, as well as the work involved in turning dreams into a reality. You showed us that big things can come from what we may perceive as being very little. As a result, I now know without a doubt that there isn't anything in this world that I can't accomplish if I want it badly enough. That is sincerely, genuinely, because of you.

As a mother, I witnessed you turn your life into a masterclass for us to learn from. I have watched you jump through hurdles, crawl in the mud, and still fight. Thank you for teaching us that challenges are not roadblocks but opportunities to grow and to rise as we have seen what you have done with a mustard seed of faith and cannot thank you enough for humbly allowing us to witness the things that most would feel are too vulnerable to share.

Your life is a testament to the message of this book, and we are so proud to be a part of your journey. Most of all, thank you for believing in me more than I believed in myself to write this foreword.

To the readers, prepare to be inspired! As you read the pages of this book, I hope you feel the same sense of inspiration and empowerment that I do when I think of Dr. Aleta Ashford. I am honored to call her my aunt and even more honored to play a small role in introducing this incredible book to the world.

The stories written in this book are more than just narratives; they are calls to action, urging us to push beyond our limits and to embrace the impossible. May this book ignite a fire within you to pursue your dreams, no matter how impractical they may seem. In sharing their experiences, the women of Beyond Limits remind us that, no matter what life throws our way, we have what it takes to rise above.

With Love & Gratitude,
Taylor S. Phew

Taylor S. Phew

Taylor Phew is the mother of three beautiful children. Born and raised in Waukegan, Illinois, she now lives in Corpus Christi, Texas. Her passion for criminal justice and helping troubled youth has led to a successful career as a juvenile probation officer for Nueces County.

Additionally, Taylor has earned a bachelor's degree in criminal justice with a concentration in Legal Studies and Advocacy from Southern New Hampshire University in 2021. Currently, she is pursuing her master's degree and remains optimistic and driven to make a difference in the lives of the youth she serves.

INTRODUCTION

In the heart of every struggle lies the potential for an extraordinary story of triumph. This book is a testament to the power of resilience, faith, and the unyielding human spirit. It is a collection of stories that celebrate the victories of women who have faced unimaginable challenges and emerged stronger, wiser, and more determined. One such story is my own.

At the age of eighteen, I ran away from home and fell into a lifestyle of addiction, unhealthy relationships, and constant searching for love in the wrong places. Methamphetamine eventually took over my life, leaving me homeless, addicted, and wandering the streets.

To simply say that meth had taken control of my life would be an understatement. I worshiped this destructive force as if it were a god, and every breath I took was in pursuit of my next high.

The turning point came when I ended up in jail and faced a judge who gave me the choice to either get my life together or go to prison. Choosing to fight for my life, I embarked on a difficult journey of recovery with God's help. While the full details of my journey are too extensive to cover here, know this: GOD fought for me and helped me overcome my addiction. The battle was won.

In 2014, I recommitted my life to the Lord and have been serving ever since. Guided by the Holy Spirit, I felt inspired to take a leap of faith to establish Thrive, Living Free Ministries—an outreach program that utilizes small group principles and relationships to spread the love and freedom that Jesus offers.

This book is not just about my journey. It is about the journeys of many women who have faced their own battles and emerged victorious. Women who remind us that no matter how dark the path may seem, there is always hope. With faith and determination, we can triumph over any obstacle.

As you read these stories, may you find inspiration and strength. May you see the power of resilience and the beauty of transformation. And may you be reminded that your story, too, has the power to inspire and change the world.

Sarah Swearingin, Thrive, Living Free Ministries

Sarah Swearingin

Sarah Swearingin currently resides in southwest Missouri where she has lived for the past decade. She has been happily married to Michael since 2019, and they have two children, Jaycee and Kaden. In her free time, Sarah enjoys gardening, and spending time with her family and friends, as well as occasionally going to a good baseball game or two.

In 2014 Sarah rededicated her life to the Lord and has been working to serve diligently ever since. As the founder of Thrive, Living Free Ministries, Sarah leads an outreach ministry that utilizes small group principles and relationship-building to spread the love and freedom found in Jesus. Her goal is to share the redemptive love of Christ with the world, as God allows. Additionally, Sarah advocates for individuals facing challenges such as substance abuse, addiction, life-controlling issues, and homelessness, collaborating with various ministries and alliances across the nation.

Joining the Grounded Jeremiah 29:11 platform in 2021 was an exciting moment in Sarah's life. Since then, she has continued in her support of Grounded Jeremiah 29:11 and is looking forward to future collaborations beyond this anthology project.

PREFACE

In a world that often challenges our strength and resilience, stories of faith and triumph serve as beacons of light. "Beyond Limits: Stories of Victory, Triumph, and Success" is a testament to the power of sharing our journeys and embracing the transformative grace of God in our lives.

As I reflect on my own path, I am reminded of the years I spent hesitating, waiting for the perfect moment to step out on faith and share my voice. What I once viewed as wasted time has become a sacred season of preparation—an opportunity for growth and development that has ultimately led me to this moment. It is within this spirit of revelation that I invite you to join me on this journey.

In September 2021, during the height of the pandemic, I was led to create Grounded Jeremiah 29:11—a faith-based women's group that blossomed from a simple desire to uplift and empower women. From its humble beginnings, Grounded has evolved into a vibrant network of ministries that not only supports personal and professional growth but also champions the Gospel of Jesus Christ. Our mission has always been to create a nurturing environment where women can share their gifts, inspire one another, and celebrate the faith that binds us.

This anthology is a culmination of those aspirations, showcasing the powerful stories of the remarkable women within the Grounded community. Each narrative is a reflection of personal challenges, triumphs, and the unwavering hope that accompanies a life rooted in faith. As you turn the pages, may you find encouragement and inspiration in the diverse experiences shared by these incredible authors.

"Beyond Limits: Stories of Victory, Triumph, and Success" is more than just a collection of stories; it is a celebration of resilience and a reminder that we are never alone in our struggles. Each voice contributes to a greater narrative of faith and solidarity, inviting readers to embrace their own journeys with courage and hope.

As we embark on this adventure together, let us remember that our stories have the power to heal, uplift, and inspire. It is my hope that these stories light a spark within you to step out in faith, knowing that God's plan for your life is filled with promise and purpose.

Dr. Aleta V. Ashford, Grounded Jeremiah 29:11

Grounded Jeremiah 29:11

Grounded Jeremiah 29:11 started as a Facebook group with fewer than twenty women at the height of a global pandemic during the fall of 2021. Today, it has grown into a virtual ministry made up of thousands of women of different backgrounds, ages, and races. What began as an outlet for inspirational quotes and scriptures has transformed into a haven that brings women together from around the world. While it is based in Orlando, Florida, Grounded has a strong following in Bolivar, Missouri, and it is represented in 43 states, Puerto Rico, and countries such as the United Kingdom, Canada, France, New Zealand, Myanmar, Thailand, South Africa, and the United Arab Emirates.

Grounded is committed to showcasing the talents, gifts, and works of Christian women and has helped dozens of women improve their branding strategies, strengthen their online presence, and create opportunities for them to connect, expand their audiences, and receive recognition. The ministry was founded by Dr. Aleta V. Ashford and continues to uplift and encourage women daily by spreading the love of Jesus Christ and sharing the stories of inspiring women who have overcome their fears and stepped out on faith to do what God has called them to do.

Since its launch, Grounded has flourished into a full-blown operation that includes a book club, anthology series, podcast, and an affiliate page highlighting the Women of Grounded. The Grounded Presents Podcast was introduced in November of 2021 and is now available on iTunes, Spotify, iHeartRadio, and Amazon Alexa.

The Grounded Presents Anthology Project launched its inaugural book in 2023, titled "Defining Moments: Stories of Strength, Courage, and Hope." This book, the first in the Grounded Presents series, is available on Amazon.com and Barnesandnoble.com.

Today Grounded continues to prioritize issues impacting women at the heart of its mission. The ministry has created an environment for women to connect, share, and exchange ideas on a wide range of topics, including faith, family, health, mental health, relationships, fitness, self-care, grief, trauma, recovery, business, marketing, and entrepreneurship.

Through its podcast, daily inspiration, and collaborations with other ministries, Grounded continues to educate, inspire, and create a positive space for women to come together and grow with God at the center of it all!

To learn more about Grounded Jeremiah 29:11 visit our website: www.GroundedJeremiah29:11.com.

The Gift of Friendship

By Dr. Aleta V. Ashford

I have often heard it said that good friends are hard to find. As I grow older, I realize just how true this sentiment is. In the hustle and bustle of my career, there was a time when I found myself struggling to keep my head above water, both professionally and personally.

My journey as a single mother had already taught me the harsh realities of life—the looming threat of unpaid bills, the constant worry of putting food on the table, and the loneliness that seemed to accompany every step I took. It was during one of the darkest periods of my life that God sent a beacon of hope that would change everything.

Being a single mother is an experience that I will never forget. Every day was a delicate balancing act, juggling the demands of work with the needs of my child. I often felt like I was walking a tightrope, with no safety net to catch me if I fell. The pressure to provide for myself and my son was relentless, and the fear of failure loomed largely in my mind. There were nights when I lay awake, staring at the ceiling, wondering how I would make it through another day.

My career, which had once been a source of pride and joy, had become a battlefield. I often felt invisible and over-shadowed by colleagues who seemed to glide effortlessly toward success while I struggled to keep up. The weight of my responsibilities was overwhelming, and I feared that I would never be able to rise above my circumstances.

In the midst of this turmoil, God provided comfort in the form of a coworker who would go on to become a trusted friend and mentor. A seasoned woman of God, she was everything I aspired to be—confident, successful, and unwavering in her faith. From the moment she entered my life, she became a source of strength and encouragement, reminding me of the power of God's word, particularly Psalm 23:5, "You prepare a table before me in the presence of my enemies".

This scripture became a mantra that I clung to in moments of doubt and despair with the understanding that my enemies were not just the people who overlooked me or the challenges that threatened to overwhelm me; they were also the fears and insecurities that were holding me back from fulfilling my purpose.

My mentor understood the struggles I faced, both as a mother and as a professional. She had walked a similar path, and her empathy and wisdom were hope for a weary soul at a time when I truly needed it.

In addition to being compassionate and encouraging, she saw potential in me that I couldn't see in myself and was determined to help me realize it by emphasizing the importance of persistence and resilience, reminding me that my struggles, while challenging were only temporary.

Life during this period was hard. Most difficult was the feeling that my son and I didn't belong to anyone. However, as I would soon learn, we belonged to God, and His love for us was beautifully expressed through this kind and loving person who consistently reminded me that I was a child of a Heavenly Father who loved me and my son.

As I grew in my faith, I was able to overcome every obstacle that came my way, including the pain of divorce, feelings of worthlessness, and emotional scars some of which took years to overcome. In Christ, I was made whole. And when faced with similar circumstances, it is important to know that God has the power to heal and make all things new.

As God began to move in my life, I found comfort in knowing that my journey was not in vain but a testament to God's transformative power. Each trial I faced became a steppingstone towards a deeper understanding of my identity in Christ, and with each new day, I grew stronger in my faith. Through prayer, reflection, and the support of my friends and mentor, I was able to let go of the past and embrace the new life God had in store for me.

The process of healing was not immediate. Instead, it required patience, perseverance, and a willingness to surrender my burdens to God. Through it all, I learned to trust in His timing and to find peace in knowing that His plans for me were far greater than anything I envisioned for myself. Eventually, my heart opened to the possibility of love, joy, and fulfillment in ways I had never experienced before.

As I reflect on this period of my life, I am reminded of the bond between Ruth and Naomi, women in the Bible who remained loyal and supportive of one another despite their differences in age and background. Their story is a beautiful testament to the power of friendship.

Ruth's devotion to Naomi, and decision to stay by her side and support her during their shared hardships, mirrors the kind of steadfast loyalty that I have been blessed to experience in my own life. The bond between them, rooted in love and mutual respect, transcended the challenges they faced and became a source of strength and inspiration.

Having experienced difficult times in my life, I am grateful for the lessons of loyalty, love, and resilience that Ruth and Naomi impart. Their relationship serves as a reminder that true friendship knows no bounds and with the support of those who care for us, we can find hope and courage to face difficulties that lie ahead.

Though I didn't realize it at the time, God had provided me with a precious gift. The gift of friendship. It was through this divine connection that I was able to heal, grow, and draw closer to God. Though the transformation from the chaos that was my life didn't happen instantly, it was profound. Slowly, the darkness overshadowing my existence began to lift, and I found myself emerging into the light.

My career, once a source of stress and anxiety, became a platform for growth and achievement. I discovered talents and strengths I never knew I was capable of, and I gained the confidence to pursue new opportunities. My son and I survived our ordeal, and as I reflect on this chapter of my life, I am filled with gratitude for the friend who appeared suddenly and stood by me in my time of need.

Today, I stand as a living testament to the power of God's grace and redemption. I am no longer defined by the struggles of my past but by the strength and purpose I have found in my faith. My journey has taught me that, with God, all things are possible (Matthew 19:26), and that His love can heal even the deepest of wounds. As I continue on my Christian journey, I hold onto the promise that God is with me every step of the way, guiding me toward a future filled with hope and possibilities.

Life's journey is not meant to be traveled alone. In the end, I have realized that good friends are not just hard to find; they are a blessing from God, sent to remind us of His love and faithfulness.

The connections we form with others can be a source of immense strength and inspiration, guiding us through the valleys and celebrating the peaks. It's in these relationships that we see the reflection of God's promise to never leave us nor forsake us, and it's in these moments of fellowship that we discover the true meaning of community.

As the founder of Grounded Jeremiah 29:11, I strive to be the example that a Godly woman once was to me. My mission is to inspire others to live boldly and confidently in the knowledge that they are deeply loved and uniquely called by God, and to create a community where women can find support, encouragement, and empowerment, just as I did when I needed it most.

I believe that by sharing our stories and experiences, we as women of God can uplift one another and grow together in our faith. It's my hope that every woman who encounters our ministry feels embraced by God's love and finds the courage to pursue her own unique calling.

Through faith, friendship, and the unwavering love of God, we can overcome any obstacle and embrace the abundant life that awaits us. As we journey together, let us be reminded that we are all part of a greater story, intricately woven by the Creator, and that each chapter of our lives holds the potential for transformation and grace.

Pearls of Wisdom:

1. Good friends are not just hard to find; they are a blessing from God.

2. The connections we form with others can be a source of immense strength and inspiration.

3. God has the power to heal and make all things new.

Dr. Aleta V. Ashford

Dr. Aleta V. Ashford is a passionate author, columnist, and inspirational speaker residing in Orlando, Florida. A devoted Christian and a loving wife and mother, Dr. Ashford is the founder of Grounded Jeremiah 29:11, an initiative that reflects her commitment to faith and empowerment. Growing up in a military environment, she has lived in diverse countries, including Germany, England, and Japan, which has enriched her worldview and inspired her writing.

With advanced degrees in Business at both the master's and doctoral levels, Dr. Ashford has dedicated much of her career to the corporate sector. Her extensive experience led her to embrace a second career as a Business Professor, where she shares her knowledge and inspires the next generation of leaders. Through her work, Dr. Ashford aims to uplift and encourage others, drawing from her life experiences and deep faith.

In Her Own Words:

There are not enough words to express all that God has done in my life in the realm of healing and restoration. Whereas I was once afflicted, God lifted my head, renewed my strength, and bestowed upon me a new name, fresh hope, and a profound sense of purpose in Him.

Embracing Today!

By Leslie Register

I t was a Tuesday that I will never forget—a day that signified the end of the old and the dawn of a new chapter in my life. In this moment, I witnessed God transforming me in ways I couldn't achieve on my own. This was the moment when light pierced the darkness of my soul, offering me a chance to begin anew.

After months of attending Alcoholics Anonymous meetings, dedicating myself to a 12-step recovery program for alcohol addiction, reading recovery literature, and conversing with other women about their journeys, I still found myself engaging in addictive behaviors. Finally, I surrendered to the truth that I was sick and needed help. My body, mind, and soul yearned for healing, and this realization was the start of my journey to overcoming addiction.

Addiction can be defined as a cycle of learned behavior in which one believes that they either can't live with or live without a particular substance or activity. From a young age, I struggled with harmful habits and coping mechanisms that held me captive. I faced eating disorders in my early teens, struggled with overspending in my twenties, and by my thirties, alcohol had become my drug of choice.

Each of these behaviors became a part of daily life, from struggling to eat food without feeling the urge to release it, to reckless spending despite having no money and pursuing career success at the expense of spending quality time with my children.

Inside, my emotions had become a battleground governed by fear, anxiety, and a numbing feeling that alcohol seemed to calm. By feeding my pain with all the wrong things, fear and anxiety continued to reign. The girl I saw in the mirror was not the woman I aspired to be, and it was then that I realized that I was the only one standing in the way of my uncovering that woman. Eventually, the pain I was experiencing compelled me to seek wellness.

My quest for recovery transcended mere sobriety from alcohol as I longed for a life free from all forms of addiction—those visible to others and the ones hidden beneath the surface. The decision I made that day started me on a pilgrimage of uncovering, discovering, and taking action that led me to freedom from the shadows of addiction. Today, I understand that all my problems and solutions reside within me, and once I chose to confront the darkness, the light emerged.

The start of my journey was uncovering the truth. This involved opening up and being honest with myself and those in my recovery circle who were guiding me on my path toward wellness. In full transparency, honesty was a concept I struggled with as I had spent much of my life telling lies or exaggerating the truth.

Choosing honesty meant that my words were truthful, and my actions were safe. Moving forward in the spirit of truth helped me to diminish fear and anxiety, allowing my authentic self to emerge from behind the veil of secrecy.

In addition to committing myself to the process of recovery, I also chose to seek God for restoration. I often say that it was God who led me to recovery, and it was recovery that brought me back to God. Although I had accepted His Salvation at age 15, I had since prioritized my own selfish desires. Now, on my recovery path, my relationship with God was renewed.

Becoming more comfortable with honesty led to my being ready to explore the "how" and "why" of my addiction as well as identifying the tools I needed to help me navigate change and the difficult journey that lay ahead.

During a visit to the hospital for alcohol abuse, one of my physicians said it best stating, "Just as you have blond hair, you also have what science identifies as an allergy to alcohol."

I had lived most of my life unaware of this condition until the "allergy" was activated through alcohol consumption resulting in an uncontrollable craving for more, despite experiencing severe consequences.

While I was genetically predisposed to having an allergy to alcohol, my addictions extended beyond a single drug or any liquid in a bottle. The root of my struggles lay in insecurities, fear, and confusion, leading me to seek anything that would help me feel better.

In my journey of recovery, I desired healing from all things. This would require a deeper exploration beyond just eliminating alcohol. This process involved seeking guidance from a therapist, attending 12-step meetings, and immersing myself in literature on trauma, people-pleasing, and eating disorders—basically anything that could foster my recovery growth.

Taking action to change was not easy! It was a blend of both messy and memorable moments. Messiness that resembled a child's first attempt at coloring within the lines or someone learning to ride a bike without training wheels, while experiencing the pain and disappointment of falling repeatedly. With a profound determination, I leaned into my thoughts, emotions, and preference for selecting new responses that I had learned throughout my recovery.

I was a 40-year-old woman when I learned to allow myself to feel my feelings, listen to my thoughts, and alter my choices from my usual patterns. Faced with anxiety and even joy while managing work, kids, and relationships, I knew wholeheartedly that I could no longer rely on food, money, or alcohol to cope.

In this discovery phase, I learned to be curious and healed from within. Transforming from a girl who at one point could only skim the highlights of a book to a woman who could read a book from cover to cover in a single day. Though I didn't quite understand it at the time, this discovery phase would become the foundation of my path toward healing.

In this new version of myself, when faced with adversity I learned to pray and ask God for guidance. I also resisted the urge to return to old habits by reaching out to those in my recovery community for advice. In some of my most challenging moments, I took walks, sometimes cried, and even learned to laugh and find humor in things.

Though it took some time, these actions would become my 'go-to' default responses. Through patience, practice, and prayer, I was able to make the transition from addiction to a new normal, embracing one day at a time.

Step 11 of the 12-Step program I participated in emphasis *"prayer and meditation to improve our conscious contact with God as we understand Him, praying only for the knowledge of His will for us and the power to carry that out."* [1] This step encourages us to engage in regular, intentional acts of spirituality, fostering a deeper awareness and relationship with God with an emphasis on praying not for personal gains or superficial desires, but for the discernment of God's will for our lives.

Aligning our recovery journey with our spiritual journey helps to reinforce a sense of purpose and inner peace. By dedicating time to prayer and meditation, we create a space for reflection and spiritual growth, which can lead to greater clarity and direction. The ultimate goal is to develop a consistent and meaningful relationship with God as He supports us in making wise, compassionate, and purposeful decisions in our daily lives.

Similarly, in Matthew 7:7, we are reminded, "Ask and it will be given to you; seek and you will find; knock and the door will be opened to you." These words are guiding principles that shape the actions and choices that

I make today. Emphasizing the importance of initiative, persistence, and faith; this scripture encourages me to take proactive steps in my life, trusting that my efforts will be rewarded and that my path will be made clear.

After years of making unhealthy decisions and relying on substances to navigate life's challenges, I now live a life where there are no limits to what God and I can accomplish together. Through God's grace and salvation coupled with choosing actions that are honest and true, I am living life to its full potential, becoming a woman that I can be proud of, and most of all I am committed to being of service to others which has helped me to focus less on my own problems.

As a survivor of addiction, I now strive to seek God in every aspect of my life. In addition to asking God for His will to be revealed, I have learned to let go. I have also learned to pause before acting impulsively, to say no when necessary, and yes when I genuinely desire to do so.

Memorable moments in recovery emerge when I make healthy choices and respond from a sober mind, body, and spirit. With each new day, I witness God's miracles unfolding in my life and the lives of those around me—miracles I would have missed out on had I not chosen to embark on the difficult journey to change!

Pearls of Wisdom:

1. Recovery is more than just stopping the addiction, it is about developing tools that help inspire critical change that enables us to do differently, think differently, and allow God to be the director of our lives.

2. While recovery is personal it is also a 'we' process. Isolation is not an option when seeking recovery as support from others is a critical key to success.

3. Recovery is not for the weak of heart or simply for those who need it. Instead, recovery is for those who want it and are willing to go to any length to get it. Recovery is work; however, the rewards are endless.

---

1. Step 11 of the 12 Step Program is a set of guiding principles outlining a course of action for recovery from addiction, compulsion, or other behavioral problems. These steps were originally developed by Alcoholics Anonymous (AA) and have been adopted by numerous other self-help and recovery groups.

Leslie Register

Leslie Register grew up in Palm Harbor, Florida, and is passionate about writing and helping people. Leslie is a curiously creative, intrinsically motivated, and spiritually guided author whose work is fueled by her faith and experiences as a successful career woman, mom, and recovering addict. Her daily prayer, "God, decrease me and increase you so I may do your will." is a reminder to cherish every moment with family and to inspire service to her community. Leslie is currently based in South Carolina where she works in commercial residential real estate, is the author of Double Shot of Sober, and a mentor to women in recovery.

In Her Own Words:

If you or a loved one are struggling with an addiction, help is available. There are over 200 12-Step recovery programs available from coast to coast. I often feel God has 'called' a select few to carry the message of addiction and recovery as evidence that while darkness exist, healing is greater. I am the evidence that recovery is possible, those who came before me showed me the way and there are people and resources available for you to also find healing.

Rising From the Shadows

By Sue Michael Carter

The journey of resilience is one that takes us through the darkest of times and challenges us to emerge stronger. My story is a testament to this transformative power. It all began when I found myself in a nursing home, a place I never imagined I'd be, stripped of privacy and consumed by feelings of helplessness and fear. The unknown loomed like a shadow, constantly whispering doubts about how long I would remain trapped in this limbo.

In those moments, I learned the profound art of adaptation. Each day was an exercise in adjusting to my new reality, a reality that was both foreign and challenging. My loss of independence was devastating, yet it was within these walls that I began to unearth the seeds of my resilience.

Pushing through the myriad challenges that life threw my way required a strength I didn't know I had. The need for knee replacements and the debilitating effects of Lyme Disease were compounded by the aftermath of three strokes. Each setback felt like a mountain, yet I was determined to scale them one by one.

Support became my lifeline. Family and friends wrapped me in a cocoon of love and encouragement, their daily visits infusing me with hope and warmth. The nursing home staff, attentive and caring, became an unexpected source of strength. In their company, I found peace and belief in knowing that I was not alone in this fight.

In the midst of these trials, I realized the importance of self-compassion. It was a valuable lesson in recognizing that healing doesn't follow a straight path; at times, the hardest yet most essential task is simply to do nothing. Meanwhile, I struggled with the frustration of not being able to walk, questioning my worth and abilities. But slowly, I learned to be gentle with myself, accepting that recovery is a journey, not a race.

Embracing patience, I understood that healing could not be hurried. It demanded time, and with this acceptance came a release of negativity. I began to identify what truly mattered, shedding the burdens of anger and resentment that weighed me down.

Creativity became my ally. When the world slept, I found comfort in the quiet of the night, engaging in physical therapy exercises that my body desperately needed. This dedication fostered a sense of control and empowerment, reminding me that I was capable of steering my own course.

Being my own advocate was a revelation. Speaking up to doctors and professionals granted me a voice and say in my own recovery that was liberating. The realization that I could influence my path instilled a newfound confidence within me.

Through this ordeal, I discovered an inner supply of strength. It was a strength that allowed me to bounce back, to find meaning in the chaos and to redefine the direction of my life. Acceptance of my new reality became a turning point, freeing me from the chains of what once was.

With this acceptance came the release of guilt and shame. I forgave myself for the decisions of the past and embraced the present with open arms. No longer did I feel the weight of what could have been; instead, I focused on the potential of what could be.

And so, I turned my focus to the future, a future bright with possibilities. This chapter of my life was not just about enduring hardship but about rising from it. It was about discovering the faith that I had within me. Faith that would guide me forward, ever resilient, ever strong.

Numbers 23:19, declares, "God is not a man that He should lie, neither the son of man, that He should repent. Hath He said, and will He not do it? Or hath He spoken, and will He not make it good."

Believing in God comes naturally when everything seems to be going great – when there's enough money in your bank account, food in the pantry, and bills paid on time. But what if you're struggling to make ends meet, with no money in the bank, no food in the cupboard, and no means to pay your bills? How can you trust in God when you're ill and everything around you seems to be falling apart?

I remember it like it was yesterday. That was the day when I heard the voice of God say to me clearly, "It doesn't matter what it feels like, it doesn't matter what your situation looks like, it doesn't matter what it sounds like. Trust me. Do not focus your eyesight on your situation, rather focus on the one who can help you overcome your situation."

It is by the grace of God that my condition wasn't as severe as a heart attack or stroke, yet life-altering no less. I was officially diagnosed with depression. An illness that often made me feel like I was in a dark cave and couldn't escape.

An illness that I was too embarrassed to tell anyone about. An illness that even after it was suggested that I seek the support of a licensed therapist or psychiatrist; I can remember thinking "There is no way in the world that I am going to see a psychiatrist or therapist." Though it took some time, eventually I saw both.

Life can be challenging, and I've certainly had my share of bad days. But through it all, I always strive to make the most of every day because I have come to understand how precious life is. I still have scars. However, I no longer allow my circumstances to hold me back. Instead, I choose to see myself as a strong, resilient woman, refined and polished by God's grace. My faith has taught me to trust God amid difficult situations, even when others don't understand my journey.

As long as I know that I am worthy in God's eyes, it is worth the sacrifice. Today I'm no longer hindered by the opinions of others. Nor do I feel shame or embarrassment when it comes to seeking professional help. Though it is God who will make me whole, I now realize that therapy is man's medical intervention that God used to heal me.

Long after leaving the nursing facility, rebuilding my motivation for my business was a challenging experience. My main source of income came from hosting live sessions online, and I was unsure how I could continue this while appearing weak and frail. Self-care became crucial as I needed to stay focused both mentally and physically.

Despite the obstacles I faced, I emerged feeling unbreakable and unstoppable. My business became a new priority, even during times when my income was limited. Instead of giving up I decided to push forward and stepped out on faith despite my fears, still ordering products with the hope of selling to regular customers and perhaps even gaining new ones.

Each week, I gained new customers, and my numbers steadily increased. Eventually, I could finally say, "I'm back." Recently, I participated in my first vending event, marking a significant milestone in my recovery and business journey.

In my personal life, regaining my independence was equally important. I started driving again, transitioning from relying on others for appointments to using a transportation service paid for by my insurance, and eventually driving myself to my many doctor appointments.

I also returned to church and began working with the Mission Ministry as well as making regular visits to a senior center, where we have lunch, play games, do chair exercises, go on outings, visit other centers, and have professionals come in to discuss current information, such as scams targeting seniors, insurance issues, and new benefits.

Living a full life, although a little differently, has been incredibly fulfilling. Despite many challenges I have embraced the mantra: "Never give up" and "Don't watch the clock; do what it does—keep moving."

While I still suffer from debilitating migraines and other health issues, I am no longer depressed. Hallelujah! When faced with difficult situations, I didn't always comprehend everything that was happening. Nevertheless, I placed my trust in the Lord. Just as I had done countless times in the past knowing that He would see me through. Without fail, God always came through for me.

"He that dwelleth in the secret place of the most High shall abide under the shadow of the Almighty, I will say of the Lord, He is my refuge and my fortress: my God; in Him will I trust." Psalm 91:1-2.

When you start living beyond the surface, there are those who may not understand your journey and may even abandon you when you don't measure up to their expectations. However, it's important to remember that God will never leave you or forsake you. For this reason, you can confidently move forward, never giving up no matter the obstacles or pitfalls that come your way.

As this chapter draws to a close, I reflect on the journey that has taken me from the depths of despair to the light of renewed hope. Though the shadows of pain and uncertainty still linger, they no longer define me. Instead, I have emerged stronger, rising above the expectations of others, holding on tight to the assurance that in Christ I am never alone.

Pearls of Wisdom:

1. Regardless of what you are going through, God has the power to heal and make you whole.

2. When it comes to your mental health, physical health, and emotional well-being, never be afraid to seek professional help.

3. Others may not understand your journey. Trust God and never give up despite the obstacles and pitfalls that come your way.

Sue Michael Carter

Sue Michael Carter, affectionately known as "Mama Sue", is a resident of Orlando, Florida. In addition to being a woman of faith, Mama Sue is a mother, grandmother, and great-grandmother as well as an overcomer who has committed a considerable portion of her life toward encouraging young women to achieve their goals.

A former caterer and owner of a daycare; Sue Michael Carter is the owner and operator of All Dolled Up Accessory LLC. and a key contributor to Grounded Jeremiah 29:11 where she takes her role as a ministry leader very seriously. Through her strength and dedication, Mama Sue has served in various areas of her community and continues to thrive and reach new heights.

Recently, Mama Sue celebrated her 79th birthday and is a gleaming example that it is never too late to pursue the plans and purposes that God has for your life.

Walking In Faith

By LouAnne M. Wischer

As the daughter of a pastor, I was taught about faith at an early age. Born with club feet, my father and grandfather—both pastors—often reminded me that God performed an immediate miracle, straightening my feet and legs after they prayed over me.

Growing up in a family that firmly believed that God could always do the impossible, I was surrounded by praying parents and grandparents. Whether it was listening to sermons in the car on a road trip or witnessing the elders in my family navigate life's highs and lows while keeping their faith in God at the forefront; I always had an awareness of God. However, when faced with some of life's most difficult challenges, my beliefs sometimes faltered, making it hard to continually walk in faith.

It was during my adulthood that I lost my father, and at that time, I found myself in a spiritually low place. Although I considered myself to be a woman of faith, my relationship with God mainly consisted of my spewing resentment and questioning His will, often leaving me closed off to the plans He had for my life.

Years later, after losing my brother, I felt bitterness take hold of my heart. Just when I thought I couldn't endure another setback, my husband and I faced challenges in trying to conceive a child. At the time I believed that infertility would be the most difficult trial I would encounter. However, through the journey of in vitro fertilization, we were blessed with our firstborn daughter, followed by twin girls just two years later.

Just as He had when I was a child, God had once again performed a miracle. For that, I felt immense gratitude and at this stage in my life, could genuinely say I had experienced God in many ways. Yet, looking back, I honestly could not say that I had a true relationship with God—at least not until that fateful day in May.

It was a beautiful day in May when I was suddenly overcome with a dreaded feeling that something was about to happen to someone in my family. Having suffered my share of loss, I did my best to push this feeling far from my mind.

A few weeks later, my husband was hospitalized for nine days due to a heart-related illness, and to make matters worse, this occurred at the onset of the global pandemic. Fortunately, I worked at the same hospital, allowing me to visit him regularly. During this challenging time, my heart began to soften, and I found myself communicating with God more. The sense of peace I experienced was beyond words, and I felt a deep assurance that everything was going to be okay.

When my husband returned home from the hospital we attended church online. In addition, I ordered a home Bible study for us to participate in with our friends and family. Little did I know that this would be the start of a ministry.

Meanwhile, my husband's condition worsened and at some point, he would return to the hospital only this time it was by ambulance. Due to a series of unfortunate events as well as a tube that had been inserted in his throat, this would be the last time I would hear my husband's voice for several months. Had it not been for the grace of God, I am not sure that I would have been able to make it through.

Scripture tells us, "For where two or three are gathered together in my name, there am I in the midst of them." This profound statement from Matthew 18:20 reassures believers that the presence of the divine is not confined to grand temples or solitary prayer but flourishes in the simple act of coming together with shared intent and devotion.

This gathering can manifest in various ways, such as on the bedroom floor where I brought our three young children together to pray for their father. It can also occur in a hospital room, particularly on the day when his room became filled with the unified prayers of visiting family and church members. In both instances, I distinctly recall experiencing the comforting presence of God enveloping the room.

Although my husband's healing journey would span across four years, I remained steadfast in my faith, grateful to God for the small miracles and blessings we experienced throughout the process. Everything, from my husband's vital signs showing improvement to the opportunity to visit him during Covid, we considered a miracle. The greatest miracle of all was how God protected our family and watched over my husband during numerous surgeries and procedures.

Having deepened my faith, I had started fasting and was dedicated to my prayer routine and Bible study by this time. Thanks to God's grace, I could pray and read the Bible to my husband each night through a speakerphone that the hospital staff kindly positioned near his ear.

Amidst the chaos and uncertainty, I began to hear God's voice more distinctly than ever before. One night, after reaching for my father's Bible, I prayed, asking God to lead me to the scripture passage He wanted me to read. It was at that moment that I opened my Bible, fully anticipating finding a verse on the topic of trusting God. Instead, I was guided to a passage about a miracle—specifically, the miracle described in Matthew 14:13-21.

This passage recounts the remarkable event of Jesus feeding five thousand people with just five loaves of bread and two fish. Not to mention, the story begins with Jesus seeking solitude after hearing about the death of John. Despite having a desire for peace, Jesus embraced the large crowd of followers who were yearning for His teachings and healing.

This miracle demonstrates Jesus's compassion and His ability to provide abundantly for those in need. For me the miracle of the fish and loaves was more than just a story. It is a testament to God's unending provision and compassion, even in the face of insurmountable odds.

Even after receiving news that my husband wasn't expected to survive an upcoming open-heart surgery, believing God for a miracle, I took my father's old Bible down to the hospital and placed it on the chest of my beloved husband. Exhausted, I prayed and worshipped God, thanking Him in advance for our miracle and for the words that He had spoken to me very clearly which were, "He will go through surgery. I will be with Him. He will recover."

I carried these words in my heart and held on to them even after my husband was placed in a long-term care facility where he remained in a comatose state for months. There were many days when I wasn't sure how or if I would survive. However, now reflecting on my journey, I see a tapestry woven by God's hand, guiding me through the darkest valleys and onto the highest peaks. Each challenge, from my childhood miracle to the trials of adulthood, is a thread in that tapestry, designed to strengthen my faith and illuminate my purpose.

On days when my heart was heavy with grief and uncertainty, God's presence was constant, gently urging me to open my heart and trust His plan. Eventually, He placed it on my heart to begin hosting online Bible studies. Not long after presenting my first series, God began speaking to me about creating a social media page called "Walking in Faith" where more than two thousand people have access to the online Bible studies that I present each month.

It was through Walking in Faith that I connected with Grounded Jeremiah 29:11, and doors have been opening ever since. In addition to being a featured speaker on the Grounded Presents podcast, God led me to start an in-person Bible study group called Dessert and Devotion. This group is made up of Christians in my local neighborhood who meet monthly to explore God's word and enjoy fellowship while indulging in their favorite desserts.

By walking in faith, I discovered that the experiences of loss, infertility, and my husband's illness were not mere obstacles, but were also opportunities for profound spiritual growth. Through prayer, fasting, and immersing myself in Scripture, I discovered a deeper relationship with God, one that transcended mere belief and blossomed into a living, breathing faith.

In the sanctuary of my home, the hospital room, and the embrace of my community, I found God's presence to be a wellspring of comfort and strength. It is through these experiences that I have come to understand my true purpose—to live a life of unwavering faith, to be a beacon of hope, and to share the boundless love and miracles of God with others.

Pearls of Wisdom:

1. Jesus always desires what is best for us, even if our lives appear to be in complete turmoil from our perspective. He has a grander plan in motion.

2. Always listen for His voice. When you take the time to seek Him, you will find Him.

3. Allow yourself to be moldable. To be like clay in the hands of the Master requires total trust in Jesus.

LouAnne M. Wischer

LouAnne Wischer grew up in Montana before relocating to Houston, Texas, after high school. A few years later, she married her husband, James Wischer. Throughout their nine years of marriage, LouAnne and James welcomed three daughters: Gracelyn, Kenley, and Kallie. Currently, LouAnne works as a registered nurse and lactation consultant, helping new mothers achieve their feeding goals. She is also the founder of Walking in Faith, where she shares Bible studies inspired by God to guide others toward Him.

In Her Own Words:

First and foremost, I want to express my gratitude to my Heavenly Father for His gentle guidance and leading in my life; I would not be here today without His presence at the center of my journey. I would also like to thank my husband of 22 years, James Wischer, for being an incredible supporter throughout the writing of this chapter and in all aspects of my life. Additionally, I am grateful to my family and friends who have prayed and supported me during this journey, particularly over the past four years. Lastly, my heartfelt thanks go to my pastor, Rev. Jason Sciscoe, for providing a strong spiritual foundation and for teaching discipleship to others.

Victory Through Adversity

By Anna L. Woods

My journey is one that I've kept close to my heart. Nevertheless, it serves as a testament to the power of prayer and the fight for spiritual, physical, and emotional wellness—an integral part of who I have become. In difficult moments, I have found solace in scripture, especially the comforting words of Psalm 23, which reminds me that even when I walk through the darkest valleys, I am never alone. This knowledge has helped me to discover peace, reinforcing my belief that victory is within reach.

Years ago, I faced a life-changing experience while giving birth to my second child. At the time, I was a healthy 40-year-old, filled with excitement and anticipation. Yet, alongside that joy was the fear of not being able to share a future with my little girl. Despite a seemingly normal pregnancy, complications arose during delivery that placed me in a fight for my life.

After giving birth, I began to lose an alarming amount of blood, and my condition rapidly deteriorated. The medical team acted quickly, performing scans and tests, but just as suddenly as it began, the bleeding stopped. I was left in a fragile state, requiring a week in the hospital to stabilize my body and regain my strength.

Throughout this ordeal, my husband and my eldest daughter were my lifeline. Their unwavering support connected me to family and friends who offered love and encouragement, helping me navigate the emotional turmoil that followed.

Looking back, I realize that my struggle wasn't just physical. Ephesians 6 reminds us "For our struggle is not against flesh and blood, but against the rulers, against the authorities, against the powers of this dark world and against the spiritual forces of evil in the heavenly realms." Despite the challenges and dangers that I faced, the power of faith coupled with the miraculous recovery that followed underscore the importance of resilience and spiritual strength in times of crisis.

Reflecting on this period, I now understand the blend of sadness and joy that came with it. The emotional journey of nearly losing my life during childbirth had simmered in the background for years, influencing my perspective on life and faith, prompting a deep reflection on my purpose and alignment. Though it was clear that God had saved me for the purpose of glorifying Him and proclaiming His name above all others, I often struggled with understanding how to live out my purpose in real-time. This challenge required me to connect emotional pain with spiritual growth and to view life's trials as opportunities for strengthening my faith.

Just as one prepares for a physical race, I had to learn to exercise my faith continuously. Even in times when I would deny emotional pain, my body kept the score. The quiet, gentle voice inside me, which I identify as my inner strength, played a crucial role in preserving my life. Listening to this voice, discerning its guidance, and taking action have been essential in overcoming internal struggles.

This same voice can be experienced through prayer as one must listen, perceive, and distinguish His voice, taking action to avoid being overwhelmed by the enemy within who prefers to see us wallow in emotional pain, obsess over it, and remain trapped. However, James 2:26 conveys a different message: "But do you want to know, O foolish man, that faith without works is dead?" As believers, it is not God's plan for us to remain stuck in emotional turmoil to the tune of letting life slip away. Instead, we can find comfort in knowing that we are victorious because of the God that we serve.

Over time I discovered that I had been carrying a lifetime of what I've come to identify as grief. It is the emotion I had buried deep within, only to resurface after my mother's death, which forced me to confront the emotional burdens I had suppressed for so long. Some burdens spanning as far back as childhood where I earned the name "Waterhead" for being a child who cried frequently. Somewhere along the way, I had learned to stifle my tears. However, through this journey, I discovered that vulnerability is not a flaw, but a vital part of our human experience as reflected in John 11, in Jesus' response to the death of his friend Lazarus.

Gaining insight into my emotions and understanding what Jesus experienced was crucial for me. I found comfort in this natural expression of grief and in knowing that He was divine yet sent as a human to experience all emotions. Accepting both joy and sadness helped me grow personally and spiritually. Recognizing that every challenge, and every moment of discomfort, could be transformed into an opportunity for growth.

Each hardship we endure is a steppingstone towards a more profound comprehension of resilience and compassion. For me personally, the process of seeking healing involved confronting my past, embracing my vulnerabilities, and finding strength in my faith. Though I never anticipated the impact of the losses I experienced, through reflection, I have found value in both the joyful and painful moments of life.

Learning to embrace my emotions, rather than running from them, has allowed me to connect with my true self and deepen my relationship with God. This newfound clarity guided me to a path where I could transform my pain into a source of strength for others.

As a life and grief coach, I now dedicate my life to empowering women to explore their emotions, heal their wounds, and discover their own purposes while motivating them to view life's transitions as points of growth and development . By sharing my story, I hope to inspire others to see their pain not as an obstacle but as a bridge to a more fulfilling life.

Since embarking on this journey, I have learned that resisting emotions only makes them harder to bear. Embracing all feelings—joy, sadness, pain—has brought me peace. While this journey isn't always easy, it has taught me that life's struggles are part of our story, and there is indeed victory through adversity.

Pearls of Wisdom:

1. Vulnerability is not a flaw but a vital part of our human experience.

2. Finding peace, purpose and victory in life's struggles requires relying on spiritual strength and perseverance.

3. Learning to view moments of discomfort as opportunities for personal growth helps to strengthen resilience.

Anna L. Woods, MMIN

Anna L. Woods has over 35 years of experience in corporate leadership, and now she is dedicated to coaching others. As a Trauma-informed Life and Grief coach she is passionate about empowering and motivating women to use life's transitions as opportunities for growth. Anna has been married to Darren Woods for thirty years, and they have four children and two grandchildren. As a blended family, they cherish each family member's uniqueness and are members of Antioch Missionary Baptist Church, volunteers in the Sunday school ministry, and other civic organizations.

After her mother's death, Anna realized that she was dealing with a lifetime of emotional pain that she had not recognized as grief. She had experienced significant losses such as miscarriage, divorce, pet loss, and two near-death events. These events had opened deep wounds that she needed to heal. Anna went on a journey of healing and self-discovery, as she drew closer to God her emotional pain provided deeper clarity into the purpose for the emotional pain.

In Her Own Words:

Thank you to my husband for his steadfast encouragement in this journey of becoming all God has created me to be.

Defining Success

By Shelby Kinuthia

How would you define success? This is an important question that everyone struggles with at some point in their lives, and the truth of the matter is that there is no correct answer. The concept of success is subjective; it varies from person to person. Therefore, each individual must determine for themselves what success looks like in order to achieve it. That's exactly what I did.

Before I begin, it's important to note the two broad definitions of success: one worldly and the other biblical. The world defines success as achieving personal goals, often resulting in wealth and fame. In contrast, the Bible defines success as obedience to God, empowered by the Holy Spirit, motivated by love for God, and directed toward the advancement of His kingdom.

As Christians, we strive to live in a way that honors God, encompassing every aspect of our lives—our hopes, dreams, and goals—because these are the elements that ignite ambition and propel us forward.

With these two definitions in mind, I chose to define success in the biblical sense. However, to understand how to set God-honoring goals and take steps toward achieving them, I had to get more specific.

Initially, I had no idea what a God-honoring goal was, let alone how to create one. But I knew where to seek answers, the Bible. God graciously provided clarity through the scripture: "For which of you, desiring to build a tower, does not first sit down and count the cost, whether he has enough to complete it?" (Luke 14:28-30). This verse guided me in the process of goal-setting.

I knew what I wanted, as that part always comes easily—it stems from our passions. My passion is performing, particularly singing in any style, group, or event. I wanted to share my God-given talents through performance. However, the approach I initially took to achieve those goals was not one I was particularly proud of.

We've all been there: "God, if you give me this, or make this happen, I promise I will...." Yet, time and again, we fall short. Eventually doubts creep in, often leading us to think, "I can't reach any goal, let alone one that honors God."

At some point it hit me! I can't achieve a God-honoring goal if I'm not living a God-honoring life. Realizing this, I understood that change was necessary. I began to pursue God actively, transforming from merely identifying as a Christian to genuinely living out my faith.

This shift moved me away from making deals with God in exchange for opportunities and achievements to working "with all your heart, as working for the Lord, not for human masters, since you know that you will receive an inheritance from the Lord as a reward. It is the Lord Christ you are serving" (Colossians 3:23-24). I recognized that success requires hard work and that if I truly wanted to achieve God-honoring goals, I needed to start living accordingly.

So, there I was living in a God-honoring way, pursuing God-honoring goals, and finally taking steps to reach success. That was up until returning to school for my senior year. On the first day, I felt nervous about what my friends would think of this new version of me. I feared being labeled a hypocrite; everyone knew my past and the sinful choices I had made. Questions swirled in my mind: "Will they think I'm a fraud?" and "Since they know the old me, will my faith mean anything to them?" You might wonder how this relates to my goal achievement.

All summer, I had eagerly anticipated using my passion for singing in our school's chapel services. Having attended a private Christian school my entire life, I had always sat in the back row during chapel. This year, however, I felt ready to take a step toward honoring God through performance. Yet the negative thoughts that sparked fear in my heart and mind nearly caused me to abandon this opportunity.

One Sunday, I attended church as I had done every week before. I sang along with the congregation and listened to the message, but that day felt different. The preacher spoke about "The devil's lies and God's truth," emphasizing that when the devil attacks us mentally and emotionally, we must counter those lies with God's truth.

I left the church that day empowered, adopting a new motto: "For God gave us a spirit not of fear but of power and love and self-control" (2 Timothy 1:7). I became aware of the spiritual battle for my soul, understanding that Satan was using my own doubts to convince me that God couldn't use me.

That Sunday, I closed the door on Satan's manipulative lies, and when self-destructive thoughts arose, I countered them with God's truth. I joined the worship team and became a chaplain—my first achievement on my journey to biblical success.

Most recently, I accomplished something I had never thought possible: I landed the lead role in my school musical. Throughout middle school and high school, I had played only ensemble or supporting roles, making this one of my proudest accomplishments. When people congratulated me, I could only respond, "Glory to God!" because this achievement was not of my doing but of His grace. God gifted me with the talent of singing and the confidence to audition, placing this opportunity in my hands to glorify His kingdom.

This journey has taught me that by setting God-honoring goals to achieve biblical success, every setback and challenge serves as a life lesson. With each obstacle, I learn to rely more on Him, empowered by the Holy Spirit to work harder and appreciate the Lord even more.

I am still on this journey to success. As I stand on the brink of adulthood, I know there is much more ahead. However, with each achievement and shortcoming, I am growing and moving closer to my goals. As I prepare to graduate and enter the world, I recognize the challenges that lie ahead. It will be difficult, but I also understand that pursuing the glory of God at the center of my success allows me to find joy even in hardships.

Everyone's definition of success is different, but when you define yours, consider who receives the glory and what others can learn from your journey. Achieving success is commendable, but the question of "How did you get there?" is equally as important as the accomplishment itself.

My hope is that one day I will be creating and performing music that glorifies God instead of drawing attention to myself. I also pray for you on your journey to success—that you honor God with your life and your goals. When you look back, may you be able to give thanks to God for guiding you every step of the way.

Pearls of Wisdom:

1. Define what success looks like for you and honor God in all things even on your journey to success.

2. To achieve a God-honoring goal, it is important to live a God-honoring life.

3. When the devil attacks mentally and emotionally, counter those lies with God's truth.

Shelby Kinuthia

Shelby Kinuthia is a high school senior from Oklahoma who participates in state choirs, her school's honor choir, jazz choir, and show choir. Additionally, she holds a position on the Student Leadership Council and serves as the Grade Level Chaplain. Shelby is a friend, a sister, and a daughter with a strong faith in the Lord. As the second oldest of four siblings, she has a deep love for her family.

In Her Own Words:

I would like to specifically thank The Lord and my Parents. I thank the Lord for never giving up on me for the countless times I went astray. He has always called me back home; even more He has blessed me immensely. I thank the Lord for His unwavering love and for making me the person I am. My parents have been my biggest supporters, making countless sacrifices to help me succeed. My greatest wish is for them to look at me and know that their sacrifices were not in vain.

God's Unwavering Love

By Tracy Ann Hamp

There was a time when I was trapped by mental and emotional struggles and bound by addiction. Yet, through God's grace and unwavering love, I have overcome these challenges and discovered my true identity in Christ.

It is through Christ that I have come to understand the profound depth of His love for me, a love that knows no bounds. It has lifted me from a place of brokenness to one of healing and restoration. Throughout my journey, I have learned that God's love is available to all, and YES, that includes you. His love has the power to change lives. No matter what challenges we face, we can find hope and strength in His unwavering love.

I am deeply grateful for the transformation He has brought into my life, and I am confident that He can do the same for anyone who seeks Him with an open heart. My story is a testament to the incredible power of God's love and how it can bring us from darkness into His marvelous light.

From the creation story in Genesis to the ultimate sacrifice of Jesus on the cross, the scriptures showcase God's grace and commitment to showering His people with everlasting love and grace. These stories serve as a reminder of God's unconditional love, forgiveness, and mercy, even in the face of our imperfections and shortcomings.

God's word emphasizes the importance of reciprocating this love by extending it to others and leading a life filled with service and compassion. These teachings remind us that, regardless of the trials and challenges we encounter, God's incredible love will always triumph, providing comfort and guidance through every facet of our lives. Thank God for that, right?

During my years of battling addiction and carrying the pain of my past along with the weight of others due to issues with codependency, God was always by my side. He revealed to me that not everyone would appreciate me, and that was perfectly fine. I realized I didn't have to alter who I am to satisfy others.

As I deepened my relationship with God, I began to see how He was transforming me from within. He reshaped my character, improved my relationships, and even revitalized my marriage.

Through this process, I finally understood His unconditional love and sacrifice for each and every one of us. He sent Himself as Jesus to make the ultimate sacrifice for our sins, even loving those who betrayed Him. This revelation of His love, forgiveness, and freedom from the grip of the enemy changed my heart completely. It made me realize that God is merciful and loving, and He doesn't exclude anyone.

By recognizing the tricks of the enemy and refusing to let him control my life any longer, I was able to break free from destructive patterns and live a life of purpose and joy. The best part is, this transformation is available to anyone who seeks it. We don't have to live in bondage anymore; we can experience the freedom and abundant life that God has promised us.

By allowing God to transform me and renew my mind, I experienced true victory. All those old habits, patterns, and struggles I had been trying to overcome for years began to fall away. I realized that I couldn't change myself and needed to trust God to do it for me. Despite still struggling with weaknesses, when I fully surrendered my heart to

Him, He spoke to me and said, "You've got it now." It was then that I understood the importance of allowing God to work on me instead of trying to do things on my own.

I have since learned that weakness is not wickedness and that God's transformation is a process. I strive to be like Jesus, to be purified and sanctified. It hasn't been an easy journey, but looking back, I can confidently say that it was worth every moment. God had warned me that the road ahead would be tough, but He promised that the end result would be worth it, and He was right.

It took me a long time to understand that God had been with me throughout all of my struggles. Having transformed from a life of addiction and prison to one of faith and renewal through God, the journey was challenging, involving trials that purified me, but I learned to surrender completely.

Just as gold is refined in fire, I emerged as a new creation, embodying the metamorphosis described in Romans 12:2: "Do not conform to the pattern of this world, but be transformed by the renewing of your mind. Then you will be able to test and approve what God's will is—his good, pleasing and perfect will". This transformation taught me to prioritize my love for God above all, including my family, leading to a better relationship with my husband.

Over time I learned to forgive myself and align my thoughts with His word, experiencing profound change. Like Paul, who endured hardships while maintaining faith, I now find strength and hope in the trials I face knowing God is always with me.

In Christ, I have come to recognize my own struggles, and perhaps you do as well. The promises found in the Bible affirm that God loves us despite our shortcomings, which is truly a blessing. Serving as a beacon of hope, strength, and comfort for believers, scriptures continually remind us that we are all cherished by God, whose love knows no limitations.

The beautiful truth conveyed in Romans 8:38-39 reassures us that nothing can separate us from God's steadfast love: "For I am convinced that neither death nor life, neither angels nor demons, neither the present nor the future, nor any powers, neither height nor depth, nor anything else in all creation, will be able to separate us from the love of God that is in Christ Jesus our Lord".

Regardless of our actions, the challenges we face, or the fears and worries we harbor, His love remains constant and unchanging. Neither death nor the powers of hell can sever the bond between us and our heavenly Father. This truth should motivate us to share God's love with others, as we possess an endless source of love and grace in Him.

May we each find comfort in knowing that we are never alone on this journey, as God's love and guidance are ever-present. Embracing this truth allows us to navigate the highs and lows of life with grace and resilience. Let us remember that every challenge we face allows us to grow deeper in our faith, leading us closer to the person we are meant to become.

Since overcoming my battle with addiction, I now serve my community by assisting individuals struggling with substance abuse, mental health challenges, and homelessness. This role stems directly from my own experiences and has been a blessing from God.

God's hand has been evident at every stage of my journey, guiding me toward growth and transformation. Through His victories in my life, He has opened doors for me to connect with others in various ways to include having the privilege of sharing my testimony of God's goodness in jails, conferences, and churches. My prayer is for God to continue to use me however He sees fit.

Despite my past as a felon, my husband and I have been blessed to foster a child and gain guardianship over him, making him our fourth son. God's blessings continue to flow through ministry, social media, and in ways I could never have imagined. I believe He will extend the same grace to everyone who puts their faith in Him.

If by chance you have not yet accepted Christ into your life, I invite you to pray this prayer with me: "Lord Jesus, I acknowledge that I am a sinner in need of Your grace. I believe that You died for my sins and rose again. I ask for Your forgiveness and invite You into my heart as my Lord and Savior. Help me to follow You and grow in my faith. Thank You for Your love and mercy. Amen."

Regardless of whether you are new to your relationship with God or have been on this path for some time, I hope that my story resonates with you. We each find ourselves at various points in our faith journey, but together, let us remain open to allowing God to work within us, transforming us into His image.

It's crucial for us to understand our identity in Christ and to speak life into ourselves and those around us. We are not just conquerors; we are also disciples of the Most High, called to put our faith into action. Together, let us claim victory and embrace the triumphs God is initiating in us and through us! All glory be to Him! Hallelujah!!!

Pearls of Wisdom

1. God's love is unwavering and extends to everyone, no matter where they are in their life.

2. Weakness is not wickedness and God's transformation is a process.

3. No matter what challenges we face, we can find hope and strength in Christ.

Tracy Ann Hamp

Tracy Hamp resides in Southwest Missouri and is a dedicated wife and mother of four children, including a foster child. She is also a proud grandmother of one.

Tracy is a strong advocate for mental health and substance abuse issues, often sharing her testimony at churches and with incarcerated women.

Co-facilitating Thrive Ministries with Sarah Swearingin has provided her purpose and joy as she witnesses its growth. As a certified peer support specialist, Tracy is dedicated to helping those struggling with addiction and inspiring others through her YouTube channel.

Guided by her faith and inspired by Jeremiah 29:11, she hopes her story encourages others to trust in God and make a difference in their lives.

Your Purpose Awaits

By Angela Salter

My story begins in a dimly lit room, where I once sat alone. With tears streaming down my face, I tightly clung to my worn Bible. Overwhelmed with sadness, my thoughts raced with feelings of worthlessness and despair as I reflected on my journey.

Life has a way of teaching some hard lessons. For me, trouble emerged when I left home as a teenager, seeking refuge from an unsafe environment. Armed with just a small suitcase and grand aspirations, I stepped into a new life in another city to live with my father. At that age, I thought I knew everything. However, as I navigated through life, I made increasingly poor decisions and found myself entangled in unhealthy relationships.

As a young woman, my involvement with a drug user led to a series of heartbreaking losses. One moment that remains etched in my memory is the funeral of my infant son, a sorrow so profound that I questioned if I would ever heal. Years later, after my oldest son was shot, it was then that I cried out to God, "Not again, please Lord... I cannot bear having to bury another child."

In the years to come time would pass in a blur of poor decisions and self-destructive behavior. Throughout these trials, I was fortunate to have parents who never ceased in praying for me. Their steadfast faith and love served as a lifeline. Even when I felt unworthy, their words and prayers sowed seeds of hope that would eventually blossom into a new life for me and my children.

One Sunday morning, I was attending church service when the minister spoke words that pierced my heart. Included in his message was the scripture, "Come to me, all you who are weary and burdened, and I will give you rest." (Matthew 11:28). It was in that moment that something inside of me shifted. I began to envision hope and prosperity for the future.

The transition between my old and new life did not come without its share of challenges. The following months were a struggle however I could feel the presence of God along the path that He was guiding me toward. Though the transformation was gradual with setbacks that often seemed impossible to overcome, I prayed fervently and did my best to focus on God's Word.

To uncover the plans God had for me, I started volunteering at church. While engaging in various ministries, I served and connected with others who like me were on their own respective journeys. This experience strengthened my faith and allowed me to hear God's voice more distinctly.

One night, I found myself deeply moved by a song on the radio that resonated with my soul. The words, "You are loved" and "His grace will carry you home..." were a catalyst for my deliverance and led to my fully surrendering to God and seeking His guidance. That night in a dimly lit room I sat alone with tears streaming down my face, clinging to my worn Bible, vowing that I would allow the Lord into my heart.

From that moment on, I set boundaries with toxic relationships, immersed myself in Scripture, and found support within a caring church community. It was then, that my life truly began to change.

I became a devoted single mother, nurturing my surviving son with faith and resilience. Though my son faced many medical challenges after his gunshot wound, he survived. Together we rebuilt our lives.

Since that fateful night in a dimly lit room where I once sat alone consumed with thoughts of worthlessness; I have grown in my faith, expanded my family to include grandchildren, and flourished in a successful career of 35 years. Most of all, I found joy and discovered my purpose in ministry and mentoring others.

It's been a long journey with peaks and valleys. However, these days when I look in the mirror at my smiling reflection, I no longer see the shame of the past that once plagued me. Instead, what I see in the mirror is an image of strength, hope, and purpose.

In closing I would like to reflect on a few words that I shared recently with a group of women at a shelter. "Though some of you may feel worthless, always remember that God has a purpose for your pain." Just as I was once lost and broken, God healed me and through His grace and mercy has the power to heal and restore those who seek Him.

Every storm you face is not meant to break you but to shape you into the person you are destined to become. Each challenge is an opportunity for growth and a step toward discovering your true potential. Embrace the journey with faith and determination while surrounding yourself with positivity.

Your story of triumph is unfolding, and it will inspire others just as much as it empowers you. Always remember that God's love is unconditional, and your purpose awaits. Therefore, keep moving forward, for brighter days are ahead, and your journey holds the promise of a future filled with joy and fulfillment.

Pearls of Wisdom:

1. God has a purpose for your pain and has the power to heal and restore those who seek Him.

2. The storms you face are not meant to break you but to shape you into the person you are destined to become.

3. Embrace your journey with faith and determination while surrounding yourself with positivity.

Angela Salter

Angela Salter is a devoted mother and grandmother who resides in Tampa, Florida. With more than 35 years of experience in the service industry and 25 years of dedicated volunteer work, Angela has made a significant impact in her community. Her faith in God, which she embraced at the age of 14, has been a guiding force throughout her life, helping her navigate both challenges and triumphs.

Angela firmly believes that facing hardships is essential for attaining the promises of God. With unwavering confidence in His guidance, she knows she can overcome any obstacle, often declaring, "God did it!"

As the founder of Pursuing Purpose Ministries, Angela is committed to spreading the Gospel of Jesus Christ and inspiring others to discover their true purpose.

A Light To Guide Us Home

By Tammy Woods

The echoes of childhood lingered in the corners of my mind, faint whispers of a time when I longed for something more than the fragmented relationships that defined my early years. Growing up in a divorced household, the longing for a connection with my father was a constant ache, a shadow that followed me into every new phase of my life.

As a child each visit to my father's home was like stepping into a different world—a world where I was an outsider, a mere visitor in the lives of my half-siblings and stepfamily, who had already woven their bonds of love and loyalty.

Despite my father's presence, I felt a distance between us, distance that often seemed impossible to bridge. The moments I spent with him were overshadowed by the tension that existed in my mother's home—a place where fear often reigned supreme.

I can still remember nights when silence was shattered by angry words, and the dread that filled me during the times I had a front row seat to witnessing the violence and abuse that often occurred in my mother's home. It was a stark reminder of the duality of my existence, caught between two households, two worlds, and two sets of emotions that often clashed.

In the midst of this dysfunction, I found comfort in the community of a church, a place where I could escape the chaos and connect with something greater than myself. I accepted Jesus Christ as my Savior at the age of fourteen, and it felt like a lifeline thrown to a drowning soul.

It was a youth pastor and his wife who became my guiding lights, introducing me to the sense of belonging I had craved for so long. In their warmth, I caught a glimpse of the possibilities of love and unity, which was a far cry from the discord I was experiencing at home.

As I entered adulthood, I carried with me the weight of my past—a mixture of resentment and hope. At eighteen, I jumped into marriage, motivated by a desire to create the family I had always yearned for.

As it turned out, I was still learning the intricacies of commitment and trust, and our union crumbled within a matter of months. The failure of my marriage deepened my sense of loss, but it also sparked a determination within me. A determination to forge a different path.

When I remarried at age nineteen, I was filled with hope. This time, I was determined to make it work. Yet, as the years unfolded, I faced the harsh reality that even the strongest desires can be tested.

My second marriage brought moments of joy, including the blessing of a beautiful daughter, but it was also marked by mistakes and heartache. Turmoil crept into our lives like a thief in the night, and I found myself struggling with the familiar feelings of betrayal and abandonment.

As I struggled and suffered through the loss of everything I had known and loved, I found myself questioning God and stopped going to church. Seeking comfort in fleeting relationships and the numbing effects of alcohol, I believed that I was in pursuit of love.

What I found instead were shadows, echoing the insecurities and traumas of my past. I felt lost, adrift in a sea of regret and self-loathing. Little did I know that God had a plan for me, a plan that would slowly unfold in ways I could never have imagined.

Even in my brokenness, I began to hear God's whispers. The words from Psalm 46:5 (NIV) reassured me, "God is within her, she will not fall..." This scripture became the thread of hope I clung to as I navigated through my struggles.

Though it took time, I learned that I was not bound by the sins and failures that haunted me. I was enough, just as I was, and coming to this realization was the catalyst for transforming my life.

Up until this point it felt like I had been wearing a mask my entire life. Somewhere along the way, the enemy led me to believe that I needed to hide. It was God, however, who revealed to me that I had been created in His image. Once I surrendered to God and began walking in obedience my life began to change.

During my journey of healing, I realized that I was enough and by the grace of God I no longer had to hide who I was. With the purpose God had given me, I was no longer captive to the mistakes of my past. The more I grew in my faith, the more I learned to forgive myself and others.

Along with a renewed sense of purpose, the decision to seek professional help was a turning point. In therapy, I unearthed the roots of my pain. My childhood traumas, particularly the day my father left which had haunted me for years, casting a long shadow over my self-worth.

I had spent decades searching for the love I had lost, feeling unworthy and alone. It was during these sessions that I started to forgive myself for the choices I had made. I realized that my past did not define me; it was merely a chapter in my story.

As I embarked on my quest for love, God sent a wonderful man who would become my husband. He was everything I had been missing as he was kind, thoughtful, and genuine. We fell in love quickly, marrying within six months. Yet, the past had a way of creeping back in, and I struggled to adapt to the new dynamics of marriage while wrestling with some unresolved issues.

Our first year was tumultuous. Arguments erupted like thunderclouds, and I found myself gravitating toward old habits and toxic relationships. The moment I filed for annulment felt like a breaking point. I was spiraling again, and the weight of my choices pressed heavily on my soul.

It was during this time that I was admitted to a psychiatric hospital, a decision that terrified and liberated me. I will never forget the sterile walls, the hum of fluorescent lights, or the moment when I realized that I was finally ready to confront my demons.

The six days I spent in the hospital was a foundation for self-discovery. It was there that I participated in group sessions, sharing my story with others who bore their own burdens. And for the first time, I felt understood. I learned to process my pain, and in doing so, I began to heal. The experience was life altering; it stripped away the layers of denial and forced me to confront the truth about my life.

Upon returning home, I decided to proceed with the annulment. I couldn't help but wonder how this man could still love me after all the hurt I had caused him. Yet, he never lost hope in me, even when I stopped attending church. While I distanced myself, he continued to attend, praying for my well-being and asking the congregation to pray for us as well.

For the first time in my life God had provided me with a partner who had the faith and wisdom to seek divine intervention on my behalf. For this, I am forever grateful to God for allowing me to experience such love. That was several years ago, and today our marriage is firmly rooted in faith.

I was well on my healing journey when I took a leap of faith to enroll in college at the age of 50. Though the thought of going back to school after so many years was terrifying, I was committed to pursuing my dreams and uncovering God's purpose for my life. Through hard work and dedication God was faithful and it wasn't long before I began to see the fruits of my labor.

While attending classes, I also worked for a nonprofit organization dedicated to helping individuals experiencing homelessness. It was then that I began sharing my testimony with others, and in return, I learned about the struggles and triumphs of people facing similar issues. It was a humbling experience, reminding me that everyone has a story, and that God has a purpose for each one of us.

By the grace of God, I went on to complete my bachelor's degree. This was a monumental achievement. I can remember walking across the graduation stage, with tears streaming down my face as I reflected on the path that had led me there. It was a poignant reminder of how far I had come, a testament to the grace and mercy of God.

Most recently I enrolled in an online master's degree program in social work while working full-time as a case manager. Though I often juggle numerous responsibilities I now have a sense of purpose. The challenges are real, but the rewards are worth it.

In addition to a healthy marriage, I also maintain a 4.0 GPA. With every passing day I feel like I am coming one step closer to fulfilling the plans God has for me.

As I reflect on this incredible journey, I realize that God has been with me every step of the way. Now walking in the fullness of His joy, I am free from the guilt and shame of my past, and I have learned to love myself as God loves me.

As if the gift of salvation and His unwavering love were not enough, God blessed me with an unexpected gift of restoring my relationship with my father. In recent years I was able speak candidly with my father who expressed having love for me, even during times when I didn't feel it. This resulted in our developing a closer relationship, and I will forever treasure the moments that we shared.

Soon after reconnecting, my father passed away unexpectedly. Although it is incredibly painful, I am grateful to God for restoring my relationship with my father and find comfort in knowing that He is with me, guiding me through my journey of grief.

Now, as I pursue my master's degree, my prayer is to honor my father's memory and to fulfill God's plan for my life. I aspire to make a difference in the lives of others, to uplift and inspire those who feel lost and broken.

Proverbs 3:5-6: reminds us, "Trust in the Lord with all your heart and lean not on your own understanding; in all your ways submit to Him, and He will make your paths straight."

With each passing day, I am filled with hope and gratitude, knowing that my journey is far from over. With each new day, I am filled with hope and gratitude, aware that my journey is far from complete.

Moving forward I will keep seeking God, embracing the blessings He has bestowed upon me while continuing to share my story with others. I am living proof that even in the depths of despair, there is a light to guide us home.

Pearls of Wisdom:

1. In Christ you are no longer captive to the mistakes of your past.

2. Never be ashamed of seeking professional help for improving your mental health.

3. Even in the darkest times find comfort in knowing that God has a plan for your life.

Tammy L. Woods

Tammy Woods is a devoted wife, mother, stepmother, and Mimi, who presently resides in Oklahoma with her husband.

A woman of faith, she has dedicated her life to Jesus Christ and to positively impacting the lives of others through her work as a therapist.

As a first-time author, Tammy is proud to contribute to the Grounded book anthology and hopes that her journey will inspire others to pursue their dreams.

ACKNOWLEDGEMENTS

The authors of Beyond Limits wish to express our gratitude to our family and friends for their encouragement and support during this journey. We also extend our heartfelt thanks to our Lord and Savior Jesus Christ for guiding this project and making the creation of this book possible.

We are incredibly grateful for the love and encouragement that has surrounded us as we embarked on this journey of sharing our stories. The prayers, kind words, and belief in our mission have been a source of strength and inspiration. Through each chapter, we hope to honor the resilience and tenacity that our readers embody, reminding them that with faith and determination, they too can triumph beyond limits.

As we release this book into the world, we are excited to see the impact it will have, touching lives and offering hope to those who seek it. Thank you for being a part of this transformative experience.

The Women of Beyond Limits

AFTERWORD

In January 2023, Grounded Jeremiah 29:11 began a year-long journey to share the inspiring stories of an incredible group of women. Collaborating completely online, Defining Moments: Stories of Strength, Courage and Hope was born. The following year the first anthology for the ministry was released and as a result ten women realized their dreams of becoming first time authors.

In January of 2024 the authors for this book began the year long journey of compiling their stories. Though a few authors were lost along the way, the group worked together as a collective to complete the project. In January of 2025 Beyond Limits: Stories of Victory, Triumph, and Success was released introducing five first time authors.

This anthology not only celebrated the individual stories of these remarkable women but also highlighted their shared experiences of overcoming adversity and breaking barriers. Each narrative was infused with a spirit of resilience and faith, demonstrating how the Gospel of Jesus Christ has been a guiding light in their lives.

As the authors navigated their journeys, they leaned on one another for support, fostering a community built on encouragement and empowerment. Group discussions, posts, and video announcements provided valuable insights into the writing process. During this process, the women evolved not only as writers but also gained the confidence to share their stories. The bonds they formed transcend the project itself, creating lasting friendships and a network of support that will continue to uplift them in their personal and professional lives.

The success of these anthologies has inspired a new wave of creativity and collaboration, as more women are stepping forward to share their stories. Grounded Jeremiah 29:11 remains dedicated to cultivating an environment where women can express their voices and share their truths, believing wholeheartedly that every story holds the power to inspire and transform.

In all these endeavors, Grounded Jeremiah 29:11 is committed to producing works that uplift the Gospel of Jesus Christ while empowering women to realize their full potential.

Dr. Aleta V. Ashford